The Forerunner

Kahlil Gibran

Table of Contents

The Forerunner

Kahlil Gibran

The Forerunner

You are your own forerunner, and the towers you have builded are but the foundation of your giant–self. And
that self too shall be a foundation.

And I too am my own forerunner, for the long shadow stretching before me at sunrise shall gather under
my feet at the noon hour. Yet another sunrise shall lay another shadow before me, and that also shall be
gathered at another noon.

Always have we been our own forerunners, and always shall we be. And all that we have gathered and
shall gather shall be but seeds for fields yet unploughed. We are the fields and the ploughmen, the gatherers
and the gathered.

When you were a wandering desire in the mist, I too was there, a wandering desire. Then we sought one
another, and out of our eagerness dreams were born. And dreams were time limitless, and dreams were
space without measure.

And when you were a silent word upon Life's quivering lips, I too was there, another silent word. Then Life
uttered us and we came down the years throbbing with memories of yesterday and with longing for tomorrow,
for yesterday was death conquered and tomorrow was birth pursued.

And now we are in God's hands. You are a sun in His right hand and I an earth in His left hand. Yet you
are not more, shining, than I, shone upon.

And we, sun and earth, are but the beginning of a greater sun and a greater earth. And always shall we be

2

the beginning.

. . . . . .

You are your own forerunner, you the stranger passing by the gate of my garden.

And I too am my own forerunner, though I sit in the shadows of my trees and seem motionless.

God's Fool

Once there came from the desert to the great city of Sharia a man who was a dreamer, and he had naught
    but his garment and staff.

And as he walked through the streets he gazed with awe and wonder at the temples and towers and
    palaces, for the city of Sharia was of surpassing beauty. And he spoke often to the passers–by, questioning
    them about their city — but they understood not his language, nor he their language.

At the noon hour he stopped before a vast inn. It was built of yellow marble, and people were going in and
    coming out unhindered.

The Forerunner

"This must be a shrine," he said to himself, and he too went in. But what was his surprise to find himself in
a hall of great splendour and a large company of men and women seated about many tables. They were
eating and drinking and listening to the musicians.

"Nay," said the dreamer. "This is no worshipping. It must be a feast given by the prince to the people, in
celebration of a great event."

At that moment a man, whom he took to be the slave of the prince, approached him, and bade him be
seated. And he was served with meat and wine and most excellent sweets.

When he was satisfied, the dreamer rose to depart. At the door he was stopped by a large man
magnificently arrayed.

"Surely this is the prince himself," said the dreamer in his heart, and he bowed to him and thanked him.

Then the large man said in the language of the city: "Sir, you have not paid for your dinner." And the
dreamer did not understand, and again thanked him heartily. Then the large man bethought him, and he
looked more closely upon the dreamer. And he saw that he was a stranger, clad in but a poor garment, and
that indeed he had not wherewith to pay for his meal. Then the large man clapped his hands and called —
and there came four watchmen of the city. And they listened to the large man. Then they took the dreamer
between them, and they were two on each side of him. And the dreamer noted the ceremoniousness of their
dress and of their manner and he looked upon them with delight.

"These," said he, "are men of distinction."

And they walked all together until they came to the House of Judgement and they entered.

The dreamer saw before him, seated upon a throne, a venerable man with flowing beard, robed
majestically. And he thought he was the king. And he rejoiced to be brought before him.

Now the watchmen related to the judge, who was the venerable man, the charge against the dreamer; and
the judge appointed two advocates, one to present the charge and the other to defend the stranger. And the
advocates rose, the one after the other, and delivered each his argument. And the dreamer thought himself
to be listening to addresses of welcome, and his heart filled with gratitude to the king and the prince for all
that was done for him.

Then sentence was passed upon the dreamer, that upon a tablet about his neck his crime should be
written, and that he should ride through the city on a naked horse, with a trumpeter and a drummer before
him. And the sentence was carried out forthwith.

Now as the dreamer rode through the city upon the naked horse, with the trumpeter and the drummer
before him, the inhabitants of the city came running forth at the sound of the noise, and when they saw him
they laughed one and all, and the children ran after him in companies from street to street. And the
dreamerÕs heart was filled with ecstasy, and his eyes shone upon them. For to him the tablet was a sign of
the kingÕs blessing and the procession was in his honour.

Now as he rode, he saw among the crowd a man who was from the desert like

himself and his heart
    swelled with joy, and he cried out to him with a shout:

"Friend! Friend! Where are we? What city of the heartÕs desire is this? What race of lavish hosts?— who
    feast the chance guest in their palaces, whose princes companion him, whose king hangs a token upon his
    breast and opens to him the hospitality of a city descended from heaven?"

And he who was also of the desert replied not. He only smiled and slightly shook his head. And the
    procession passed on.

And the dreamerÕs face was uplifted and his eyes were overflowing with light.

Love

    They say the jackal and the mole
    Drink from the self–same stream
    Where the lion comes to drink.

    And they say the eagle and the vulture
    Dig their beaks into the same carcass,
    And are at peace, one with the other,
    In the presence of the dead thing.

O love, whose lordly hand
Has bridled my desires,
And raised my hunger and my thirst
To dignity and pride,
Let not the strong in me and the constant
Eat the bread or drink the wine
That tempt my weaker self.
Let me rather starve,
And let my heart parch with thirst,
And let me die and perish,
Ere I stretch my hand
To a cup you did not fill,
Or a bowl you did not bless.

The King–Hermit

They told me that in a forest among the mountains lives a young man in solitude who once was a king of a
vast country beyond the Two Rivers. And they also said that he, of his own will, had left his throne and the
land of his glory and come to dwell in the wilderness.

And I said, "I would seek that man, and learn the secret of his heart; for he who renounces a kingdom
must needs be greater than a kingdom."

7

The Forerunner

On that very day I went to the forest where he dwells. And I found him sitting under a white cypress, and
in his hand a reed as if it were a sceptre. And I greeted him even as I would greet a king.

And he turned to me and said gently, "What would you in this forest of serenity? Seek you a lost self in
the green shadows, or is it a home–coming in your twilight?"

And I answered, "I sought but you — for I fain would know that which made you leave a kingdom for a
forest."

And he said, "Brief is my story, for sudden was the bursting of the bubble. It happened thus: One day as I
sat at a window in my palace, my chamberlain and an envoy from a foreign land were walking in my garden.
And as they approached my window, the lord chamberlain was speaking of himself and saying, 'I am like the
king; I have a thirst for strong wine and a hunger for all games of chance. And like my lord the king I have
storms of temper.' And the lord chamberlain and the envoy disappeared among the trees. But in a few
minutes they returned, and this time the lord chamberlain was speaking of me, and he was saying, 'My lord
the king is like myself — a good marksman; and like me he loves music and bathes thrice a day.'"

After a moment he added, "On the eve of that day I left my palace with but my garment, for I would no
longer be ruler over those who assume my vices and attribute to me their virtues."

And I said, "This is indeed a wonder, and passing strange."

And he said, "Nay, my friend, you knocked at the gate of my silences and received

8

but a trifle. For who
   would not leave a kingdom for a forest where the seasons sing and dance
ceaselessly? Many are those who
   have given their kingdom for less than solitude and the sweet fellowship of
aloneness. Countless are the
   eagles who descend from the upper air to live with moles that they may know the
secrets of the earth. There
   are those who renounce the kingdom of dreams that they may not seem distant from
the dreamless. And
   those who renounce the kingdom of nakedness and cover their souls that others may
not be ashamed in
   beholding truth uncovered and beauty unveiled. And greater yet than all of these is
he who renounces the
   kingdom of sorrow that he may not seem proud and vainglorious."

   Then rising he leaned upon his reed and said, "Go now to the great city and sit at its
gate and watch all
   those who enter into it and those who go out. And see that you find him who, though
born a king, is without
   kingdom; and him who though ruled in flesh rules in spirit — though neither he nor
his subjects know this; and
   him also who but seems to rule yet is in truth slave of his own slaves."

   After he had said these things he smiled on me, and there were a thousand dawns
upon his lips. Then he
   turned and walked away into the heart of the forest.

   And I returned to the city, and I sat at its gate to watch the passersby even as he had
told me. And from
   that day to this numberless are the kings whose shadows have passed over me and
few are the subjects
   over whom my shadow passed.

The Lion's Daughter

Four slaves stood fanning an old queen who was asleep upon her throne. And she was snoring. And upon
the queen's lap a cat lay purring and gazing lazily at the slaves.

The first slave spoke, and said, "How ugly this old woman is in her sleep. See her mouth droop; and she
breathes as if the devil were choking her."

Then the cat said, purring, "Not half so ugly in her sleep as you in your waking slavery."

And the second slave said, "You would think sleep would smooth her wrinkles instead of deepening them.
She must be dreaming of something evil."

And the cat purred, "Would that you might sleep also and dream of your freedom."

And the third slave said, "Perhaps she is seeing the procession of all those that she has slain."

And the cat purred, "Aye, she sees the procession of your forefathers and your descendants."

And the fourth slave said, "It is all very well to talk about her, but it does not make me less weary of
standing and fanning."

The Forerunner

And the cat purred, "You shall be fanning to all eternity; for as it is on earth, so it is in heaven."

At this moment the old queen nodded in her sleep, and her crown fell to the floor.

And one of the slaves said, "That is a bad omen."

And the cat purred, "The bad omen of one is the good omen of another."

And the second slave said, "What if she should wake, and find her crown fallen! She would surely slay
us."

And the cat purred, "Daily from your birth she has slain you and you know it not."

And the third slave said, "Yes, she would slay us and she would call it making a sacrifice to the gods."

And the cat purred, "Only the weak are sacrificed to the gods."

And the fourth slave silenced the others, and softly he picked up the crown and replaced it, without
waking her, on the old queen's head.

And the cat purred, "Only a slave restores a crown that has fallen."

And after a while the old queen woke, and she looked about her and yawned. Then she said, "Methought I
dreamed, and I saw four caterpillars chased by a scorpion around the trunk of an ancient oaktree. I like not
my dream."

Then she closed her eyes and went to sleep again. And she snored. And the four slaves went on fanning
her.

And the cat purred, "Fan on, fan on, stupids. You fan but the fire that consumes you."

Tyranny

Thus sings the She–Dragon that guards the seven caves by the sea:

"My mate shall come riding on the waves. His thundering roar shall fill the earth with fear, and the flames
of his nostrils shall set the sky afire. At the eclipse of the moon we shall be wedded, and at the eclipse of
the sun I shall give birth to a Saint George, who shall slay me."

Thus sings the She–Dragon that guards the seven caves by the sea.

The Saint

In my youth I once visited a saint in his silent grove beyond the hills; and as we were conversing upon the
nature of virtue a brigand came limping wearily up the ridge. When he reached the grove he knelt down
before the saint and said, "O saint, I would be comforted! My sins are heavy upon me."

And the saint replied, "My sins, too, are heavy upon me."

And the brigand said, "But I am a thief and a plunderer."

And the saint replied, "I too am a thief and a plunderer."

And the brigand said, "But I am a murderer, and the blood of many men cries in my ears."

And the saint replied, "I too am a murderer, and in my ears cries the blood of many men."

And the brigand said, "I have committed countless crimes."

And the saint replied, "I too have committed crimes without number."

Then the brigand stood up and gazed at the saint, and there was a strange look in his eyes. And when he
left us he went skipping down the hill.

And I turned to the saint and said, "Wherefore did you accuse yourself of uncommitted crimes? See you
not this man went away no longer believing in you?"

And the saint answered, "It is true he no longer believes in me. But he went away much comforted."

At that moment we heard the brigand singing in the distance, and the echo of his song filled the valley
with gladness.

The Plutocrat

In my wanderings I once saw upon an island a man—headed, iron—hoofed monster who ate of the earth and
drank of the sea incessantly. And for a long while I watched him. Then I approached him and said, "Have
you never enough; is your hunger never satisfied and your thirst never quenched?"

And he answered saying, "Yes, I am satisfied, nay, I am weary of eating and drinking; but I am afraid that
tomorrow there will be no more earth to eat and no more sea to drink."

The Greater Self

This came to pass. After the coronation of NufsibaŠl, King of Byblus, he retired to his bedchamber — the
very room which the three hermit–magicians of the mountains had built for him. He took off his crown and his
royal raiment, and stood in the centre of the room thinking of himself, now the all–powerful ruler of Byblus.

Suddenly he turned; and he saw stepping out of the silver mirror which his mother had given him, a naked
man.

The king was startled, and he cried out to the man, "What would you?"

And the naked man answered, "Naught but this: Why have they crowned you king?"

And the king answered, "Because I am the noblest man in the land."

Then the naked man said, "If you were still more noble, you would not be king."

And the king said, "Because I am the mightiest man in the land they crowned me."

And the naked man said, "If you were mightier yet, you would not be king."

Then the king said, "Because I am the wisest man they crowned me king."

And the naked man said, "If you were still wiser you would not choose to be king."

Then the king fell to the floor and wept bitterly.

The naked man looked down upon him. Then he took up the crown and with tenderness replaced it upon
the king's bent head.

And the naked man, gazing lovingly upon the king, entered into the mirror.

And the king roused, and straightway he looked into the mirror. And he saw there but himself crowned.

War and the Small Nations

Once, high above a pasture, where a sheep and a lamb were grazing, an eagle was circling and gazing
hungrily down upon the lamb. And as he was about to descend and seize his prey, another eagle appeared
and hovered above the sheep and her young with the same hungry intent. Then the two rivals began to fight
filling the sky with their fierce cries.

The sheep looked up and was much astonished. She turned to the lamb and said:

"How strange, my child, that these two noble birds should attack one another. Is not the vast sky large
enough for both of them? Pray, my little one, pray in your heart that God may make

16

peace between your
    winged brothers."

And the lamb prayed in his heart.

———

Critics

One nightfall a man travelling onn horseback towards the sea reached an inn by the roadside. He
dismounted, and confident in man and night like all riders towards the sea, he tied his horse to a tree beside
the door and entered into the inn.

At midnight, when all were asleep, a thief came and stole the traveller's horse.

In the morning the man awoke, and discovered that his horse was stolen. And he grieved for his horse,
and that a man had found it in his heart to steal.

Then his fellow–lodgers came and stood around him and began to talk.

And the first man said, "How foolish of you to tie your horse outside the stable."

And the second said, "Still more foolish, without even hobbling the horse!"

And the third man said, "It is stupid at best to travel to the sea on horseback."

And the fourth said, "Only the indolent and the slow of foot own horses."

Then the traveller was much astonished. At last he cried, "My friends, because my horse was stolen, you
have hastened one and all to tell me my faults and my shortcomings. But

strange, not one word of reproach
     have you uttered about the man who stole my horse."

Poets

Four poets were sitting around a bowl of punch that stood on a table.

Said the first poet, "Methinks I see with my third eye the fragrance of this wine hovering in space like a
    cloud of birds in an enchanted forest."

The second poet raised his head and said, "With my inner ear I can hear those mist–birds singing. And the
    melody holds my heart as the white rose imprisons the bee within her petals."

The third poet closed his eyes and stretched his arm upwards, and said, "I touch them with my hand. I
    feel their wings, like the breath of a sleeping fairy, brushing against my fingers."

Then the fourth poet rose and lifted up the bowl, and he said, "Alas, friends! I am too dull of sight and of
    hearing and of touch. I cannot see the fragrance of this wine, nor hear its song, nor feel the beating of its
    wings. I perceive but the wine itself. Now therefore must I drink it, that it may

sharpen my senses and raise
me to your blissful heights."

And putting the bowl to his lips, he drank the punch to the very last drop.

The three poets, with their mouths open, looked at him aghast, and there was a thirsty yet unlyrical hatred
in their eyes.

The Weather–Cock

Said the weather–cock to the wind, "How tedious and monotonous you are! Can you not blow any other way
but in my face? You disturb my God–given stability."

And the wind did not answer. It only laughed in space.

The King of Aradus

Once the elders of the city of Aradus presented themselves before the king, and besought of him a decree
to forbid to men all wine and all intoxicants within their city.

And the king turned his back upon them and went out from them laughing.

Then the elders departed in dismay.

At the door of the palace they met the lord chamberlain. And the lord chamberlain observed that they were
troubled, and he understood their case.

Then he said, "Pity, my friends! Had you found the king drunk, surely he would have granted you your
petition."

Out of My Deeper Heart

The Forerunner

Out of my deeper heart a bird rose and flew skywards.

Higher and higher did it rise, yet larger and larger did it grow.

At first it was but like a swallow, then a lark, then an eagle, then as vast as a spring cloud, and then it
   filled the starry heavens.

Out of my heart a bird flew skywards. And it waxed larger as it flew. Yet it left not my heart.

   . . . . . .

O my faith, my untamed knowledge, how shall I fly to your height and see with you man's larger self
   pencilled upon the sky?

How shall I turn this sea within me into mist, and move with you in space immeasurable?

How can a prisoner within the temple behold its golden domes?

How shall the heart of a fruit be stretched to envelop the fruit also?

O my faith, I am in chains behind these bars of silver and ebony, and I cannot fly with you.

Yet out of my heart you rise skyward, and it is my heart that holds you, and I shall be content.

Dynasties

The queen of Ishana was in travail of childbirth; and the King and the mighty men of his court were waiting in
breathless anxiety in the great hall of the Winged Bulls.

At eventide there came suddenly a messenger in haste and prostrated himself before the King, and said,
"I bring glad tidings unto my lord the King, and unto the kingdom and the slaves of the King. Mihrab the
Cruel, thy life–long enemy, the King of Bethroun, is dead."

When the King and the mighty men heard this, they all rose and shouted for joy; for the powerful Mihrab,
had he lived longer, had assuredly overcome Ishana and carried the inhabitants captive.

At this moment the court physician also entered the hall of Winged Bulls, and behind him came the royal
midwives. And the physician prostrated himself before the king, and said, "My lord the King shall live for
ever, and through countless generations shall he rule over the people of Ishana. For unto thee, O King, is
born this very hour a son, who shall be thy heir."

Then indeed was the soul of the King intoxicated with joy, that in the same moment his foe was dead and
the royal line was established.

Now in the city of Ishana lived a true prophet. And the prophet was young, and bold of spirit. And the King
that very night ordered that the prophet should be brought before him. And when he

was brought, the King
   said unto him, "Prophesy now, and foretell what shall be the future of my son who is this day born unto the
   kingdom."

And the prophet hesitated not, but said, "Hearken, O King, and I will indeed prophesy of the future of thy
   son, that is this day born. The soul of thy enemy, even of thy enemy King Mihrab, who died yester–eve,
   lingered but a day upon the wind. Then it sought for itself a body to enter into. And that which it entered into
   was the body of thy son that is born unto thee this hour."

Then the King was enraged, and with his sword he slew the prophet.

And from that day to this, the wise men of Ishana say one to another secretly, "Is it not known, and has it
   not been said from of old, that Ishana is ruled by an enemy?"

Knowledge and Half–Knowledge

Four frogs sat upon a log that lay floating on the edge of a river. Suddenly the log was caught by the current
   and swept slowly down the stream. The frogs were delighted and absorbed, for never before had they sailed.

The Forerunner

At length the first frog spoke, and said, "This is indeed a most marvellous log. It moves as if alive. No
such log was ever known before."

Then the second frog spoke, and said, "Nay, my friend, the log is like other logs, and does not move. It is
the river that is walking to the sea, and carries us and the log with it."

And the third frog spoke, and said, "It is neither the log nor the river that moves. The moving is in our
thinking. For without thought nothing moves."

And the three frogs began to wrangle about what was really moving. The quarrel grew hotter and louder,
but they could not agree.

Then they turned to the fourth frog, who up to this time had been listening attentively but holding his
peace, and they asked his opinion.

And the fourth frog said, "Each of you is right, and none of you is wrong. The moving is in the log and the
water and our thinking also."

And the three frogs became very angry, for none of them was willing to admit that his was not the whole
truth, and that the other two were not wholly wrong.

Then a strange thing happened. The three frogs got together and pushed the fourth frog off the log into
the river.

The Forerunner

"Said a Sheet of Snow–White Paper..."

Said a sheet of snow–white paper, "Pure was I created, and pure will I remain for ever. I would rather be
burnt and turn to white ashes than suffer darkness to touch me or the unclean to come near me."

The ink–bottle heard what the paper was saying, and it laughed in its dark heart; but it never dared to
approach her. And the multicoloured pencils heard her also, and they too never came near her.

And the snow–white sheet of paper did remain pure and chaste for ever — pure and chaste — and empty.

The Scholar and the Poet

Said the serpent to the lark, "Thou flyest, yet thou canst not visit the recesses of the earth where the sap of life moveth in perfect silence."

And the lark answered, "Aye, thou knowest over much, nay thou art wiser then all things wise — pity thou
canst not fly."

And as if he did not hear, the serpent said, "Thou canst not see the secrets of the deep, nor move among
the treasures of the hidden empire. It was but yesterday I lay in a cave of rubies. It is like the heart of a ripe
pomegranate, and the faintest ray of light turns into a flame–rose. Who but me can behold such marvels?"

And the lark said, "None, none but thee can lie among the crystal memories of the cycles: pity thou canst
not sing."

And the serpent said, "I know a plant whose root descends to the bowels of the earth, and he who eats of
that root becomes fairer than Ashtarte."

And the lark said, "No one, no one but thee could unveil the magic thought of the earth — pity thou canst
not fly."

And the serpent said, "There is a purple stream that runneth under a mountain, and he who drinketh of it
shall become immortal even as the gods. Surely no bird or beast can discover that purple stream."

And the lark answered, "If thou willest thou canst become deathless even as the gods — pity thou canst
not sing."

And the serpent said, "I know a buried temple, which I visit once a moon: It was built by a forgotten race

of giants, and upon its walls are graven the secrets of time and space, and he who reads them shall
understand that which passeth all understanding."

And the lark said, "Verily, if thou so desirest thou canst encircle with thy pliant body all knowledge of time
and space — pity thou canst not fly."

Then the serpent was disgusted, and as he turned and entered into his hole he muttered, "Empty–headed
songster!"

And the lark flew away singing, "Pity thou canst not sing. Pity, pity, my wise one, thou canst not fly."

Values

Once a man unearthed in his field a marble statue of great beauty. And he took it to a collector who loved all
beautiful things and offered it to him for sale, and the collector bought it for a large price. And they parted.

And as the man walked home with his money he thought, and he said to himself, "How much life this
money means! How can anyone give all this for a dead carved stone buried and

undreamed of in the earth
     for a thousand years?"

     And now the collector was looking at his statue, and he was thinking, and he said to himself, "What
     beauty! What life! The dream of what a soul!— and fresh with the sweet sleep of a thousand years. How can
     anyone give all this for money, dead and dreamless?"

Other Seas

     A fish said to another fish, "Above this sea of ours there is another sea, with creatures swimmming in it —
     and they live there even as we live here."

     The fish replied, "Pure fancy! Pure fancy! When you know that everything that leaves our sea by even an
     inch, and stays out of it, dies. What proof have you of other lives in other seas?"

Repentance

On a moonless night a man entered into his neighbour's garden and stole the largest melon he could find and
brought it home.

He opened it and found it still unripe.

Then behold a marvel!

The man's conscience woke and smote him with remorse; and he repented having stolen the melon.

The Dying Man and the Vulture

Wait, wait yet awhile, my eager friend.
I shall yield but too soon this wasted thing,
Whose agony overwrought and useless
Exhausts your patience.
I would not have your honest hunger
Wait upon these moments:
But this chain, though made of breath,
Is hard to break.
And the will to die,
Stronger than all things strong,
Is stayed by a will to live
Feebler than all things feeble.

The Forerunner

Forgive me, comrade; I tarry too long.
It is memory that holds my spirit;
A procession of distant days,
A vision of youth spent in a dream,
A face that bids my eyelids not to sleep,
A voice that lingers in my ears,
A hand that touches my hand.
Forgive me that you have waited too long.
It is over now, and all is faded:—
The face, the voice, the hand and the mist that brought them hither.
The knot is untied.
The cord is cleaved.
And that which is neither food nor drink is withdrawn.
Approach, my hungry comrade;
The board is made ready.
And the fare, frugal and spare,
Is given with love.
Come, and dig your beak here, into the left side,
And tear out of its cage this smaller bird,
Whose wings can beat no more:
I would have it soar with you into the sky.
Come now, my friend, I am your host tonight,
And you my welcome guest.

Beyond My Solitude

The Forerunner

Beyond my solitude is another solitude, and to him who dwells therein my aloneness is a crowded
   market–place and my silence a confusion of sounds.

Too young am I and too restless to seek that above–solitude. The voices of yonder valley still hold my
   ears and its shadows bar my way and I cannot go.

Beyond these hills is a grove of enchantment and to him who dwells therein my peace is but a whirlwind
   and my enchantment an illusion.

Too young am I and too riotous to seek that sacred grove. The taste of blood is clinging in my mouth, and
   the bow and the arrows of my fathers yet linger in my hand and I cannot go.

Beyond this burdened self lives my freer self; and to him my dreams are a battle fought in twilight and my
   desires the rattling of bones.

Too young am I and too outraged to be my freer self.

And how shall I become my freer self unless I slay my burdened selves, or unless all men become free?

How shall my leaves fly singing upon the wind unless my roots shall wither in the dark?

How shall the eagle in me soar against the sun until my fledglings leave the nest which I with my own beak
   have built for them?

The Last Watch

At high tide of night, when the first breath of dawn came upon the wind, the Forerunner, he who calls himself
echo to a voice yet unheard, left his bed–chamber and ascended to the roof of his house. Long he stood and
looked down upon the slumbering city. Then he raised his head, and even as if the sleepless spirits of all
those asleep had gathered around him, he opened his lips and spoke, and he said:

"My friends and neighbors and you who daily pass my gate, I would speak to you in your sleep, and in the
valley of your dreams I would walk naked and unrestrained; for heedless are your waking hours and deaf are
your sound–burdened ears.

"Long did I love you and overmuch.

"I love the one among you as though he were all, and all as if you were one. And in the spring of my heart
I sang in your gardens, and in the summer of my heart I watched at your threshing–floors.

"Yea, I loved you all, the giant and the pygmy, the leper and the anointed, and him who gropes in the dark
even as him who dances his days upon the mountains.

"You, the strong, have I loved, though the marks of your iron hoofs are yet upon my

32

flesh; and you the
   weak, though you have drained my faith and wasted my patience.

"You the rich have I loved, while bitter was your honey to my mouth; and you the
poor, though you knew
   my empty–handed shame.

"You the poet with the bowed lute and blind fingers, you have I loved in
self–indulgence; and you the
   scholar ever gathering rotted shrouds in potters' fields.

"You the priest I have loved, who sit in the silences of yesterday questioning the fate
of my tomorrow; and
   you the worshippers of gods the images of your own desires.

"You the thirsting woman whose cup is ever full, I have loved in understanding; and
you the woman of
   restless nights, you too I have loved in pity.

"You the talkative have I loved, saying, 'Life hath much to say'; and you the dumb
have I loved,
   whispering to myself, 'Says he not in silence that which I fain would hear in words?"

"And you the judge and the critic, I have loved also; yet when you have seen me
crucified, you said, 'He
   bleeds rhythmically, and the pattern his blood makes upon his white skin is beautiful
to behold.'

"Yea, I have loved you all, the young and the old, the trembling reed and the oak.

"But, alas, it was the over–abundance of my heart that turned you from me. You
would drink love from a
   cup, but not from a surging river. You would hear love's faint murmur, but when love
shouts you would muffle
   your ears.

The Forerunner

"And because I have loved you all you have said, 'Too soft and yielding is his heart, and too undiscerning
is his path. It is the love of a needy one, who picks crumbs even as he sits at kingly feasts. And it is the
love of a weakling, for the strong loves only the strong.'"

"And because I have loved you overmuch you have said, 'It is but the love of a blind man who knows not
the beauty of one nor the ugliness of another. And it is the love of the tasteless who drinks vinegar even as
wine. And it is the love of the impertinent and the overweening, for what stranger could be our mother and
father and sister and brother?'

"This you have said, and more. For often in the market—place you pointed your fingers at me and said
mockingly, 'There goes the ageless one, the man without seasons, who at the noon hour plays games with
our children and at eventide sits with our elders and assumes wisdom and understanding.'

"And I said, 'I will love them more. Aye, even more. I will hide my love with seeming to hate, and disguise
my tenderness as bitterness. I will wear an iron mask, and only when armed and mailed shall I seek them.'

"Then I laid a heavy hand upon your bruises, and like a tempest in the night I thundered in your ears.

"From the housetop I proclaimed you hypocrites, pharisees, tricksters, false and empty earth—bubbles.

"The short—sighted among you I cursed for blind bats, and those too near the earth I likened to soulless
moles.

34

The Forerunner

"The eloquent I pronounced fork–tongued, the silent, stone–lipped, and the simple and artless I called the
  dead never weary of death.

"The seekers after world knowledge I condemned as offenders of the holy spirit and those who would
  naught but the spirit I branded as hunters of shadows who cast their nets in flat waters and catch but their
  own images.

"Thus with my lips have I denounced you, while my heart, bleeding within me, called you tender names.

"It was love lashed by its own self that spoke. It was pride half slain that fluttered in the dust. It was my
  hunger for your love that raged from the housetop, while my own love, kneeling in silence, prayed your
  forgiveness.

"But behold a miracle!

"It was my disguise that opened your eyes, and my seeming to hate that woke your hearts.

"And now you love me.

"You love the swords that stroke you and the arrows that crave your breast. For it comforts you to be
  wounded and only when you drink of your own blood can you be intoxicated.

"Like moths that seek destruction in the flame you gather daily in my garden: and with faces uplifted and
  eyes enchanted you watch me tear the fabric of your days. And in whispers you say the one to the other,
  'He sees with the light of God. He speaks like the prophets of old. He unveils our souls and unlocks our

hearts, and like the eagle that knows the way of foxes he knows our ways.'

"Aye, in truth, I know your ways, but only as an eagle knows the ways of his fledglings. And I fain would
disclose my secret. Yet in my need for your nearness I feign remoteness, and in fear of the ebb tide of your
love I guard the floodgates of my love."

After saying these things the Forerunner covered his face with his hands and wept bitterly. For he knew in
his heart that love humiliated in its nakedness is greater than love that seeks triumph in disguise; and he
was ashamed.

But suddenly he raised his head, and like one waking from sleep he outstretched his arms and said, "Night
is over, and we children of night must die when dawn comes leaping upon the hills; and out of our ashes a
mightier love shall rise. And it shall laugh in the sun, and it shall be deathless."

CPSIA information can be obtained
at www.ICGtesting.com
Printed in the USA
LVHW061617270622
722145LV00032BA/21

9 781169 193802